Sasha Sings the Laundry on the Line

Sasha Sings the Laundry on the Line

poems by
Sean Thomas Dougherty

American Poets Continuum Series, No. 125

BOA Editions, Ltd. ⁂ Rochester, NY ⁂ 2010

Manufactured in the United States of America

First Edition
10 11 12 13 7 6 5 4 3 2 1

Publications by BOA Editions, Ltd.—a not-for-profit corporation under section 501 (c) (3) of the United States Internal Revenue Code—are made possible with funds from a variety of sources, including public funds from the New York State Council on the Arts, a state agency; the Literature Program of the National Endowment for the Arts; the County of Monroe, NY; the Lannan Foundation for support of the Lannan Translations Selection Series; the Sonia Raiziss Giop Charitable Foundation; the Mary S. Mulligan Charitable Trust; the Rochester Area Community Foundation; the Arts & Cultural Council for Greater Rochester; the Steeple-Jack Fund; the Ames-Amzalak Memorial Trust in memory of Henry Ames, Semon Amzalak and Dan Amzalak; and contributions from many individuals nationwide. See Colophon on page 80 for special individual acknowledgments.

Cover Art and Design: Sandy Knight
Interior Design and Composition: Richard Foerster
Manufacturing: Thomson-Shore
BOA Logo: Mirko

Library of Congress Cataloging-in-Publication Data

Dougherty, Sean Thomas.
Sasha sings the laundry on the line : poems / by Sean Thomas Dougherty.
— 1st ed.
p. cm.
ISBN 978-1-934414-39-2
I. Title.
PS3554.O8213S27 2010
811'.54—dc22

2010009201

BOA Editions, Ltd.
250 North Goodman Street, Suite 306
Rochester, NY 14607
www.boaeditions.org
A. Poulin, Jr., Founder (1938–1996)

Contents

for Lisa, my last love

"Or if I told you
that it was not a seam
but a doorway
to the otherside—"

—Malena Mörling

"My landlord never heard of me
and expects his rent just the same
as he expects it from the junkies"

—Franz Wright

"I wanted to sing the great arias with you."

—Carol Maso

1

Arias

Pavarotti is dead and the streets are full of arias,
    my brother. Every window a tenor leans,

there are sopranos in the olive branches.
    And all across the globe the world

turns to crescendos. Along Parade Street the day passes.
    The Russian women lean on their steps, discussing

the price of cabbages. The boys with tattoos
    ride their skateboards, skipping curbs,

and there is a music to their wheels, a screech,
    a scat and scatter, a turntable cutting *La Bohème.*

Pavarotti is dead and the streets of his hometown
    are full of weeping, and as his casket is carried

the people's voices speak, as when Verdi died,
    and as they carried him through the streets

the people spontaneously began to sing
    the slave song of the Hebrews from *Nabbuco.*

All the dead are rising through the olive branches.
    The elms are weeping on Parade Street

where the sunlight is the color of opera.
    Where my hands are holding my face,

watching the television, the streets full
    of the crowd, gathering to give witness

to what burned their chests and told them
    the true name of sorrow. When we weep

we are most alive. I turn off the television
    and listen to Sasha upstairs. I hear her steps

dancing to a Russian pop song's staccato.
    There are arias everywhere, my brother.

Can you hear them ghosting through the laundromat steam,
    with the clack of cue balls in the pool halls,

at the CITGO station when the gas glugs,
    where one-legged Jethro waits outside

on the curb, humming while smoking a cigarette?
    He blows a halo of smoke casually into the air,

it swirls, composes notes and disappears,
    like a song, a kind of blessed noise, the way music

enters us and vanishes. What remains is why we live.

2

The House of Fragments

That year of nothing but *weeping*
Over pirogues for breakfast at Dombrowkis,
Your grandfather crossed the river
Back to the old country.
The spires of cathedrals we'd count,
Driving through the snow
To nowhere. Ukrainians in leather caps playing poker
At the back of the Pinochle Club.
Like the silhouettes of wild dogs
In alleyways. It was the year those children
Disappeared and they found the man
In a basement and he had an *accident.*
The year the police shot how many Black boys dead.
But this is more about *desire*,
Mangoes on a plate, the Monongahela we swam in,
Through condoms and detritus
We dove through the green murk,
Like discarding whole doctrines.
Then the shifts grew. I loaded,
You waited. *Weighted*, but what wind?
The frozen lake, the fields of corn
We ran in naked, through the grape vines.
Nights in the rooms of distilled voices,
A riff lisped with piano keys
In the jukebox's pleading.
High on chocolate martinis. Slurry on vodka tonics
In a tall glass. Justin talked of catching a freighter
For the summer. Hauling
Anthracite across Lake Erie.
Your grandfather's ghost photos from the mines
In Poland, then the baking and the bread

For the Jewish bakery, and your father
Riding in the bread truck to church.
The broken wings of birds, glued together.
The stillness of the snow, *like a toothache*
The old Russian man said. Walking
His great black dog along the bay.
Like a great bear, through the great stillness,
Covering the ice. The grief song
Gabriel blows, the weathervane spinning
Above Malichevskis garage.
Where is this all going, you ask? Back to you tracing
The scars above my eyebrows,
One thin finger, you naked
Except for your turquoise tank top.
And the words like accidents,
Or ornaments. What we said or were afraid
To confess, like winter itself,
And the freezing rain slicking the roads black.
Who doesn't return?
From the warehouses and the factories
Now husks, you stealing copper
From the closed-down paper plant,
Trading it for dope,
Trading found cans. Or the hours
When she doesn't come home
In the morning. The Lackawanna, the Reading
She said, *like the cards from Monopoly.*
Trains hauling by with their graffiti, blue
And silver whole car murals gleaming.
Old men fishing beside RVs. *Everywhere*
Is elsewhere but here.
Until the city of closed-down steel
And rusted water
Reveals its razored wings.

The young boys slinging rocks began to sing
The prisms that hide in the air.
City of what part of you is going.
City of what is inside You begins to bruise.
Torn mattresses in vacant lots, stranger's kneeling.
A box cutter waved in the fat man's face.
Weaving the sunlight, praying
In fumes, hustling outside the truck stop by the interstate.
Who disappeared?
Abandoned by the side of the road,
Brown-bagged kittens. *Your mother weeping*
In her gray dress. *Lonely as a river.*
The pick-up trucks of Spanish grape-pickers,
The one with the guitar standing,
What they are saying you can almost translate:
Like seeing a body rise to the surface
Of the quarry, before it sinks again.

~

And then what matters? That city is so far away, and he is
drowned,
The one you ran with. And the other is asleep this night of moon
Behind another cell. And she is signing to her deaf mother, before
putting on
Rouge, to sing in the dives, to *shush.* And nothing matters but
looking
In the right direction down the tracks, and the pocks on her face
are healing.
And the scars she's given herself, and her bare shoulders
and the wind
That smells of garlic and weaves the starlings through the black
trees. You sip
Your coffee strong, dark as dirt. This insomnia a blue glow
behind battered windows.

To live there and here. Without disclosure or confession, But the slant of light,
Or a certain scent: gardenias, tulips, lilacs. The funerals forgiven, the failures
Or her voice to return. The anger is an ancient script that must become *hieroglyphic*.

~

And then you see the sky has opened over the skyline, and you are
Sobbing for the reverie of the birds. The *reverie* of a broom
Sweeping the way he moved. The janitor lifting
His head. And then there are those evenings when everything ruined is revealed
In the stillness of the snow, or the ushering of the rain, guiding you through the theater
Of blocks where you used to know people, of the city of night and
Refugees. The oboe player in the high window above Slomski's
Funeral parlor. The weight of this music. Lilting with string.
What is seamstress but a form of grieving? Sewing the black
Seams. Sewing whiskey drank shot and the moon above the refinery plant. Sewing
The rain into a shawl the babushkas wear, carrying bread. Sewing
The taxis of yellow light as they ride empty through the city of
Sorrowful songs. The sorrowful songs
Of whiskey and the rain and why she is gone, *he is dead*. The radio sewing the wind,
Sewing the walls between rooms where insomnia pins the eyes. Walking through
The house of fragments. Nothing is whole.

Subterranean Waltz

Beneath the train trestle, a hooded boy spray-paints a roof, a prism of city glass, a blurring of wings. The hushed hiss of his Krylon can: the B-boys' lullaby. A beat is the night's whirring with the sirens blocks spreading red and blue braids of light. The night's camouflage a fierce calligraphy. The admission price for the moon erased. A radiant billboard sells a soft mouth. Rouged. Mascaraed. Her pain caged brightness, and the profit of loss. Or a catalogued opening, unconcealed, she calls down a passing car. Where rooms of mourning are lined with someone singing to a silhouette or exhaustible stare at the wall. Practicing the waltz with headphones. So late even the neon is asleep. Who can weep over the sudden snowfall? Except M. In the eaves trough of unknown strands of memory, a hornet's nest of regrets buzzes in his brain. He lifts the basement shade, blows a cigarette's worth of smoke under the cracked storm window. On his forehead, M has the amplitude of a Death notice posted on the last room in the hall. The vertigo of a winding stair. The white moths of the snow fill the air. He reaches under the screen to touch the fluttering wings, like an evangelist. Wishing he could become a piano. They become the notes he couldn't see—*M, for once, you aren't afraid.* His worn-down nails, even full of pills and booze, his hands still move, pressing the keys on the table, his jeans. *What is ugly*, M says, *music will destroy.* M forges fugues: M forgets to breathe.

After

The small story that begins with a girl
never swinging on a backyard swing,

dangling her long braids,
a boy never riding his scooter

and singing a nonsense song,
pushing with his bare feet:

wordy birdie dirty birdie.
The wind moving the hairs on my arm

like human breathing.
A blue jay stealing eggs

in the boysenberry tree.
The shadows asleep in their beds.

And then the garbage can
I bent to lift up, covered with maggots.

So I pulled it out to the sun
and by late afternoon

they were white husks, the finches pecking
the last ones for the nestlings' upturned mouths.

And the green flies that swarm to eat the berries
offer a hum that turns the air iridescent.

I want to offer you a set of wings,
instructions to play a cello,

but all I can give you is the chalk
a child left on the sidewalk.

Or a dragon-tailed kite
flying on a string so long it rises

over the tenement roofs,
higher than the hospital

where the helicopter
emergevacs the near dead.

At the CITGO station I look down
at a shimmering puddle of gas.

At the Lebanese market
where I do not turn away

from the lamb's head
hanging in the window.

At its bulbous eye, at my own face
reflected in its black pupil:

There Is No Idea Here

A bag of flour in your grandmother's kitchen. The chiaroscuro somewhere of kisses. Sentiment, *so What.* No clue or neatly played. This is a threaten against cut rate. A pick up against the easily sublimed. Who suffers, shrank in the heat of observation. No one is listening. Sasha is asleep, my neighbor who sings laundry on the line. When it flaps I hear symphonies. She steps with Prokofiev in her step, or is that Justin Timberlake blasting *I'm bringing sexy back.* SO what? The sun still gleams gold off the Orthodox dome. There is beauty here like the old country, the old women, babushkaed (I say it again) kneeling on their knees on the steps, speaking in the mother tongue. Peep Jesse with his tatoots, his mad tats, seventeen and sanguine, looking a bit stoned on no one to fuck, he's got his mofoing electric remote control car doing wheelies in the street, sixteen inches of Bling Bling brake! Even the old women are entranced. Is it that? Like a shrug, or a sigh, or as Jim writes a simple nod? Could it be that easy? Down at Michalchevski's the drunks are at it again, betting ones on who wins what or loses when. What is illuminated but this ballroom, this border I cross, the nowhere else but where. The nations gather, lose what they've run from, the terror, the dread, there are no death squads, no police tonight, the neighborhood boys are lounging, playing spades or dice, the old women kneel as if praying, speaking Russian like an abstract graffiti, the Cyrillic alphabet marking manifestos in the allegorical air.

At the Intersection of Parade and Punk

Gogol Bordello contrapunting gypsy punk accordion
as I'm weighted unemployed at the red light, watching
the Day Laborers lined up waiting
for their call outside the DAY EMPLOYMENT door
in the near-closed plaza except for a RENT TO OWN
and the DAY OLD Donut Shop, (not its real name,
but every time we've gone there the donuts were stale).
The men in line are all wearing fingerless gloves,
bubble coats, fur-lined parkas, camouflage,
they are all smoking, and waiting, waiting
for the door to open to earn a day's wages,
a day's work, a day's bread.
On a day that it is cold out,
the kind of cold that kills,
the kind of cold where some kid sledding
always finds a man frozen in the park dead.
Bordello now is blowing, the accordion
and the violin and the drum and the bass line
weaving threads, and I roll down my windows
and let the sound rise as the light turns green
and the music wafts turning a few heads,
perplexed glances, when one white brother
about my age raises his fist. And we all should
be praying over a screeching guitar riff,
praying for everyone raking minimum-wage,
and all the nightshifts, loading trucks
with the heft of our hands, lifting the boxes
of things to the ceiling with the forklift's limbs,
the forklifts lifting all the foreign-made-things,
all the world's things packed in bubble wrap
and cardboard pressed from the pulp of trees

like the limbs of our callused hands,
like the man I played pool with who had three fingers,
two cut off by a stamping machine, last night he spit
into his palms and lined the pool cue over the absence
of his fingers and ran the table five times—Randy
was his name—he and his friends all in their fifties,
weather-shorn but steel-hard and razor-ribbed,
razor-winged men who worked with their hands,
and now I am driving the punk music blasting.
There is graffiti in the sky, and somewhere else it is still dark
and a man bends to tie his boots, to punch a punch card,
and somewhere there is a lifetime of shredding,
the documents of the dead, the bread
that must be given, as when the workday is done,
and the boss drops you off to walk home
through the gloaming, as you did from the dirt lot
or the ball field when you were a child,
how before you gripped anything, you spit into your hands.

Untitled

Friday Happy Hour and the paychecks are cashed at every corner store so gracefully a fish hangs in a Chinese shop window a somewhere morning factory nervousness erased so gracefully the downpour of digging the road crews leaning on their shovels the whistle of the press repairmen what can they afford still reaching for the other's tab a transvestite in the bar beyond the refinery dances in place so gracefully sips a martini mandolins in the background of a country jukebox song cacophony of pool balls colliding the train tracks down twelfth street mythic the napkins rolled after her shift a waitress so gracefully eating dope on a second-floor fire-escape in early spring the crocuses croon the daffodils swoon the junkies nod their wilting heads so gracefully stoop-shouldered so beautiful

The Opposite of Elegy

When you were strung out

and I kissed you
I imagined your mouth

a mound of cocaine,
inhaling your breath

like powder as I pushed
into you and you pulled

me with your bruised thighs.
Some nights we fucked so

slowly I dissolved
like a Quaalude in a glass

of vodka, and you drank
me down. We kept the room dark,

so we could not see
each other with our eyes

rolled back—or was it
because we did not want

to see ourselves.
It's taken me too long to think

of that, the way we never
thought the other would go,

and then one night
I woke up

sober
and yes,

still there.

My Neighbor Shadrack Has Been Coughing All Night Again

He sits on his stoop and drinks. He is high on something I cannot name. This is not the start of a story. I want to live by betraying nothing. Yesterday a fly landed on the page of my open book. I felt less alone then. The dark clouds were gathering over the lake. Once, the factory machines told me the hours of my day. When I wake I have nowhere to go. At the death of Lao Tsu, Chin Shih chastised the old saying they were grieving as if for their children, the young as if for their mothers. To live without joy or grief, the spirit a fire that burns long after the wood is gone. An old man coughing at night sends his voice across the street. A fly touches the page: A flying word. Without grief there is nothing to cure us. In the factory, I'd stare at the turbines spinning like Dervishes. The noise devoured our names. We wore earplugs. We were voiceless, arms, legs, lifting and feeding the machines. There is no argument here, no moral, no parable. Only a cello. Maybe a swallow. These round words to dive into. The robin pulling the worm. When it sings, the cat pricks up its ears. If there is a you it is mirrored. Meteor showers. The music of fucking. If I could give you a purpose I would map you my losses. Spell you the language of splinters. I am so poor all I have to eat is an old man coughing. In the ravishing dark, you must believe nothing vanishes

Untitled

"My absence has left me today"
—M

My absence has left me today.

I have gone nowhere.

The sheets hold my body. At the corner

where I would have waited for the bus,

my absence waits. At the library,

how many books of literature

remain untouched? My absence

you see, is smarter than me,

he is there reading

about electromagnetic engineering,

genetics, the syntax of the Mayan language.

My absence has loved many women well.

But that is History.

Today my absence has left me.

When he returns to the room, he will say

I have been everywhere and you must step

out of the shadows. But you are my shadow,

I will say, when you are not here,

when you are out in the world traveling,

it is the abscess of you

I can feel swallowing me whole.

Dear Tiara

I dreamed I was a mannequin in the pawnshop window
 of your conjectures.

I dreamed I was a chant in the mouth of a monk, saffron-robed
 syllables in the religion of You.

I dreamed I was a lament to hear the deep sorrow places
 of your lungs.

I dreamed I was your bad instincts.

I dreamed I was a hummingbird sipping from the tulip of your ear.

I dreamed I was your ex-boyfriend stored in the basement
 with your old baggage.

I dreamed I was a jukebox where every song sang your name.

I dreamed I was an elevator, rising in the air shaft
 of your misgivings.

I dreamed I was a library fine, I've checked you out
 too long so many times.

I dreamed you were a lake and I was a little fish leaping
 through the thin reeds of your throaty humming.

I must've dreamed I was a nail, because I awoke beside you still
 hammered.

I dreamed I was a tooth to fill the absences of your old age.

I dreamed I was a Christmas cactus, blooming in the desert
of my stupidity.

I dreamed I was a saint's hair-shirt, sewn with the thread
of your saliva.

I dreamed I was an All Night Movie Theater, showing the
flickering black reel of my nights before I met you.

I must've dreamed I was gravity, I've fallen for you so damn hard.

Ode and Elegy to the Sound of My Lover Peeing

Someone else has written an ode to the sound
of their lover peeing, I think it was Creeley, who is dead,
who I went to Helsinki to write an ode to, him dead
far from I-90 and that big house that would gather the young,
to drink wine over words and bread. Now this is a different
    sound/
lover (L) from my last lover (E), though I remember E peeing,
the quiet stream of it, the way Creeley wrote of his lover (   )
all I can put are parentheses because I can't remember *the*
    language,
the way in Helsinki in the blue light surrounded by the dying
    alcoholics
I could not find the language to write of Creeley,
for the anger between E and I on the street, anger like the teeth
of the giant pike, the skeleton of the giant pike her uncle hung
from a hook out on the archipelago I believed something was
    eaten
away from, eaten from us, from me, verbs and the sound of the
    rain, the sound
of the little boat's engine that took us from shoal to shoal, the
    sound
of drunks dying in the alleys of Helsinki, the way we were dying,
the way Creeley died on a bed in a blue room in Odessa, Texas,
far from Finland and the Baltic Sea in spring on the other side of
    the world
where we died, or here in the breaking light where my lover is
    peeing,
and what I feel for her is like dying, is like the sound of someone
    torn

being sewn.

Sewn with new thread. Gold thread, the thread some woman
in the old country might have sewn into a funeral shawl
for someone quiet and brave as Robert Creeley, and E's face,
how it is hard to even find as I write this for the sound
of her voice was such a torrent, a waterfall
shattering shutters and L's voice, humming
from the bathroom, as she wipes and flushes, this sound,
the before sound of her peeing, the quiet hush of it,
like the sound of weeping, like the sound
of someone putting a finger to the lips of someone weeping,
the way L touched my face when I was frail, and took me past
    language,
which is what Robert Creeley did. Which is why we miss him,
which is how I miss L, from the next room. It is the difference.
When she is peeing. When the sound stops. What I wish for you.

Our Love as an Origami Crane

Kiss me as Björk sings the discordant swoon-light,
searchlights ghost across our bodies' banks.

Ankle to hand, the illusionists we've become
tongues struck to the dark wind.

Pin the mute flywheel you feel,
peel back your raiment. Björk cracks sound,

rounds vowels we open in a field,
yielding a harvest beyond despair—

repair, nothing we bear shall ever harden into fists.

What We Were Given

What we were given, no more than
the architecture of a hand holding a hand.
Shards of glass we gathered on the lake shore.
The tiny cut on my thumb you sucked.
Her eyes of sleeping doves on the bus.
The lighter burns on your arms:
Paleolithic scars, pale ancient moons.
In the small of our backs: winged palms.
There is no touching if we turn away.
There is no grieving except what we accept.
At the rest stop where you squatted to piss.
There is no story we can tell, you said.
Only fragments, half-forgotten faces,
a tapestry of what could have been.

What could have been a tapestry to hang
when grandfather walked through the gloaming
after his long shifts. When the refinery whistle
whistled and the Twelfth Street train rumbled
coal past the open panes of tenement windows.
When the tea kettle steamed,
steamed through the walls and no one stopped it.
When the spring sky was full of kites,
but the only bird she found was wounded.
When the fish die when the ice breaks,
and the stink rises, and the children
bend to touch their silvered skin.
When the waitress leans on her elbows,
her short hand, her sorrowful shine.

The sorrowful shrine
of the ones leaving and the ones left,

stitching their crosses
and crescents across our chests.
Wounded in the bare rooms
underneath a bare bulb,
farmhouses with one candle
lit, such symphonies
rising out of the summer
lawns: against this grief
the tiny Beings began to sing—
not laments—but arias
asking for each other
inside the urgent dark.

The urgent dark where we waited
for what to hold to arrive,
the way we leaned into each other
learning not to be alone, or when I was inside you
your hands fit so perfect in the small of my spine.
Or was it your eyes drunk with August,
my scars you mapped with your tongue—
and then she arrived, tiny as a winter plum,
with our palms we lifted her to the lamplight,
and she grew and the I-remember-whens
began to sing, to hum, to holler as she ran home down the block
to eat, bowing our heads, for no one but the three
of us, and the small rooms where we asked
for nothing more than what we were given.

3

Arbitrary Cities

> *"Or maybe it's a carnival we hire onto,*
> *our bodies stitching together*
> *arbitrary cities."*
>
> —John Rybicki

Gulag of clay and shit and longing, gulag
  of stitches and songs. Across borders,

latitudes, barbed wire, where no one can
  understand your tongue, where the constellations

shift, of blue lightmares where you draw the sky's
  figures, like clouds. Like children coloring

clouds. Like translating the light off a river
  on the day your grandfather died,

remember almost drowning in the grief
  of your own two hands, the two folded prayers,

folded like your summer clothes, or a mortgage bill
  your father hid from your mother until

the house was sold. The gulag of sold things,
  tomatoes and tomatoes and your sister

Sasha, your sister you said, back in Azerbaijan,
  how they promised her a job as a waitress

in Virginia, sent to Prague
  along the highway the gulag of bordellos

and slaves, and the German "sex tourists," that gulag
    of broken flint, that gulag of crushed fingers

and cut-off cocks—let us send THEM to that gulag
    Sasha, far from this gulag along the frozen lake,

and the gold-domed cathedral
    gleaming. Sasha, can you hear

the gulag of trumpets and the men who interrupt
    and the rumors of translations and the mute

children missing and the woman behind me
    who says, *everything that is broken is blessed.*

~

Dear Sasha,

there is a blue bottle broken by the gutter
of our apartment house on Parade Street,
on the edge of the blue light lilted frozen lake,
a bottle blue as blue lake glass, ice blue its song
its ice blue broken song, this stolen prayer,
how neither of us will lift it to our lips like a flute
and blow a song for the children
playing hopscotch on the sidewalk
next summer on a day no one was shot,
a song for the blackbirds gliding
over the frozen fields, fields
like in the black earth
of our ancestors and the black-earthed bones
of our dead. Sasha, how many songs
are such broken things?

The losings you carry in your own chest?
Your stuttered words, your unsaid answers
I can tell are more than lack of translation,
how your mother, old seamstress, rests
in the second-floor window and sends a sigh
down into the street, a sigh so heavy
even the wind bows over the broken dandelions
in the backyard, a sigh stitched
with what one cannot forget: earth, bones,
a door that once opened never does. O Sasha,

is there a song
that can save us?
A song
for the arbitrary shanties,
the run-down tenements
of Sixth Street where the white rock sweats
The Palm's hands
the jeweled bloods,
redheads drinking Jack Daniels,
something to conjure more than a tiara.
O Sasha, a song that is delirious,
uncompromised, and elementary
as the black earth sending its sunflowers
first sprouting their black-faced suns.

A song like a tongue,
that touches the nape of the neck,

like milkweed along the train tracks
when I was a child, a thousand tiny saints
in white shrouds like my grandfather's hands
holding me in the dim light of what was shape
and pour like rain and sleep like drowse. Sasha,

at night when your radio plays, the Russian pop songs, the teenage love-ballads, sometimes I hear the shuffle of soles and know that you are dancing with yourself, like breath across the page of a book, I can hear you orbiting in the near-dark, white moth to the green light of the CD player's dial, can hear the far-off snore of your father who never says a word, who sometimes stands in his great fur hat on the porch staring off at nothing I can see, not looking down or up but straight ahead, as if he hears such a concerto, a violin, an oboe in the wind that his heart is held in a gloved or glorious fist! What can save us but such sound? Or are we drowning? O Sasha,

for whatever you have witnessed,
I have seen you in your sorrow
in the backyard, with the basket of clothes

by your bare ankles, seen you kneel down and become
stuck, you cannot stand, staring at a daddy longlegs
crawling in the grass that you mistakenly

crushed, and such sudden and unexpected grief
as you began to weep I felt ashamed to watch,
and then just as sudden you rose to sing

the laundry line of notes, humming the sound
that might be the frequency a distant quasar
makes as it is born.

~

Or maybe the grass,
when it finally slumbers for the long winter?

Or the wind when it is most still, the hum that rises from the bodies of strangers as they wait in the cold for the bus and one opens his mouth and they begin to talk, the simple talk of living, of what did we do and where are we going today, and there is a hum to human voices when they merge when the words become simply sound: *round mound pound clowns laughing bathing fountains spray stray dogs all day* it gathers this hum this profound alphabet never-written. O Sasha,

    it is getting late. The arbitrary cities
of our lives will go on long after I am gone

from this two-story tenement on the edge
    of the frozen lake in this rusty town

of abandoned factories and cheap dinors,
    will shine like the deaf who sign

    Karaoke to each other at Coaches' Bar. Sasha,
if you were old enough you could go

    when the hush of your house was too loud
and no song you play could be enough,

and watch them as they sign: the lack of sound
    is the ancient language

of sighs between the stillness

of the night sky and the nails

of light that pierce our bodies

with their brilliant, noiseless words—

Without Making a Noise

The map of the mountain that can mistake the loneliness from which it comes. Not clarity or the silent blues, like a harmonica, the man plays whiskey. The man blows the map into Being. Being that for three months I rode a bus. I rode the rust. Of my seventh birthday. My dog shot dead. Dead, down the hill he rolled with a hole in his chest. A handful can be a lifetime. A handful of seconds he was sprawled beside me on the white man's lawn. He told the police, *Damn dog pissed on my grass.* Where is the map to erase this, a long journey passed our dead? My friends: Garry drowned in a quarry. Jolie dead of cancer. Shaun in Walpole State Prison. Brucie in a Nevada Prison. Roger in a Tennessee Prison. Why expand? You know the story. Drugs, federal statutes, mandatory five years. Gun possession. This is America I tell my Bosnian friend. Lewisburg, Attica, Rikers Island where my uncle got clean. Flex at Concord State Prison. How many prisons? How many missing? Dead? The sound of prisoners sleeping. Regie who shot another boy in Mattapan. Or Suzanne's college roommate murdered by her ex-boyfriend. The obituaries we carry. A six-inch article. One day's news. As if looking through a swinging window. A boat's window? Is that why it moves? So many of us Charon has been replaced. The steam blows my life's intimate doubt, greased courage. Grease at the kitchen, washing dishes, grease of too many lost shifts, lost wages, lost jobs, the woman who couldn't teach, her name was Terri, I told her to go fuck herself, that language I had in my head. Some things you shouldn't say, the incompetent channels, the victimized stance: *these American white women, professionals who read your poems, drink Bourgeoisie bourbon, wrapped in their Victorian tongues, as if a century of genocide does not make their complaint's ephemeral.* Someone told me this: My Bosnian friend Ermina, when she speaks of there, she climbs the mountain: Beautiful ladder out of hell. She said, *what to them is my best friend raped, murdered, the Serbs cut off her limbs. Her name was Tatjana. What to them?* She sipped her coffee. A map of blue tulips bloomed around the well. Do we spade our grief and speak, stammering without embarrassment, speak the blueprint of a grace to give away? Wouldn't that be swell. But Ermina and I sat there without speaking, without touching. Burn the institutional walls, burn the bad tongues. In the quiet rooms of my building of refugees, sometimes there is an almost-sound, like the echo of someone weeping through the walls. Sometimes there is nothing to be said. Ermina pointed, reaching, outside the coffee-shop window, starlings were swooping their black notes across the sky: transient, tremulous—

X

X Vietnam Vets with shotguns and six-packs, fingering shells
after watching *The Deer Hunter.*

X cops pushing mops, X machinists laid off after twenty hard
years, drinking

straight shots of Jack, buying 50 cent drafts with counted dimes.

X cafeteria workers and coal smoke. Who ain't broke? Who ain't
X'd?

Who ain't waiting for that last severance check?

Who X'd out twilight at the plant gate, ghost towns and gutters
and two inch pipes.

X the broken traffic light in burnt-out Toledo. On the corner
some woman waiting in the rain for nothing we can name.

You dig it, X marks the spot. What else she got? What else she
forgot about her skin?

X on the cap on my Pops, tilted sideways still cool like he's
copping a fro and long sideburns.

X on the sidewalk where bleeding Billy Montgomery laid down
and said, "Please walk my dog."

X sleepwalkers listening to Slovenian Polka as Wittgenstein
Scholars pass out pamphlets, Xtra Xtra rhythm swiveling,
skeleton suits in the dark Museum of Irrational American
History.

X operators still sticking digits in the air above their hospital beds,
milky white cataract eyes. Who takes the minimum wage to
change their bed pans, hold their fingers as they tremble?

Can you dig this? Can you dig the dying and the dead? Dig into
the X-Files to find the forgotten and the grieven, the lost
causes undercut by FBI agent provocateurs? You think
the government don't have the cure, locked in a secret cabinet
meeting? Wild-haired bitter academics talking about Hegemony—

Did you ever think that you're the enemy? With your obfuscating
lingo? Have you ever witnessed the old women talk and
smoke at BINGO? The beauty of their brash ashes?

When you walk on my block, I'll jack your thesis (just more
feces).—don't believe this? You're funded by Guggenheim;
I'm funded by wind chimes and cheap wine, carpenter's nails
and Kool-Aid.

Let us begin again, X is X filling the world with evening prayers
poured slowly in a cool glass.

X is a DJ named gravity who speaks in the language the color of
charity. Says Marry Me.

X gangbangers along the Los Angeles basin the graffiti spells *Dia
De Muerto.*

X voices that spill through subway shadows, what elegy what
slow child named Sorry, what sixties funk, what rhymes with
physician?

Can I get an X-ray Doctor?

Named J.

Rising from the far foul line: recognize his dissonance, the distance between Schoenberg and Psychedelic Funk is seconds not centuries.

X-out nostalgic riffs for the spark of spliffs and grifted gliss. This is more than spit. This is a manifesto

to toe (repeat to infinity).

A J for Joe

J is the first letter of my dead grandfather's name.
I could pin a J to my office door but what of it—
Why only a single letter memorial?
Instead, I could stick a J from the far corner, let it rise
like a blue jay from a branch as I cry Joseph,
which is the name for another father.

The priests let the incense hover
like the smoke from a J,
the one my boy Paul lit
at a party in Lowell, the night we got
arrested & ended up in a Lawrence cell, & Manny
bent over crying for everything we never told.

J as in Jam Master jamming on the cassette
in my '72 Chevelle, through the black glass night
J is the first letter of Jehovah, of Johnstown, PA
where the flood waters rose high as Noah,
where my friend A jogs at night,
to jettison the JuJu her last lover
carved into her spine.
J as in Jersey, the small bodega
where Joe and I woofed red fish & rice
after teaching tenth graders.
We sat out in the Spanish night
smoking menthols—

as fifteen-year-old girls pushed strollers, chatting
in El Salvadoran accents, the street of saffron
& sofrito, soccer balls & sequined letter chains—

not saying anything, except listen with our eyes
as the city turned blue & the streetlights turned yellow
& some girl hollered out a window, “Hey J—”

How her voice hung in the air, as if it was tattooed,
as if it was burned inside us.

Raphael

The refinery smoke thick in the East Side air, like eating gravel when I inhale, and I pass the bar called Scotty's where you sang gravel-voiced and off key to me, toasting with that expensive Scotch, lifting your arm high above the jukebox's illuminated disks, that bar where we drank the smoke of the refinery, of lost shifts, of nights lost on those humid days and the small rooms in the hotel where we spent those years living on nothing but words and the dark liquid that we drowned in.

To drown, we didn't, or did we? Even now I find myself swimming towards the one light, the bare bulb swinging in the banished rooms, the rooms where we danced, two brothers, to a radio seeping out of an open window in the widow's house, where she swayed in her black-veiled Otherness, in the loss of her man in Guatemala or El Salvador or someplace like Ecuador, where I hear the red bananas hang above the outstretched arms of the dead, she of the long weepings. She could never let go, like so much we didn't

ask or say? Raphael, my brother, your wings were made of razors, sharp as the blade you carried in your back pocket, just in case, you said, in case you had to, and once, I thought when you walked in with blood on your hands I thought you had, but it was the blood from the fish you caught on the East Side pier, the one you said fought so hard you wanted to throw it back, the lake bass who swam so deep and long you thought it was me.

Me who swam with you through so many nights the city forgot its own name, and we became just City, street, corner block, pool hall, Brother, all the simple words that sing the rain's lullaby.

That sing goodbye, that sing forgive me, like that widow muttering in Spanish, in the high window across from the building where we ended up, and the Russian landlord named Yevgeni, like Yevtushenko the great laureate, the dark language he spoke from Siberia, and the winters of the freezing rain, and the autumns of the sudden snow, where the black leaves silhouette the sidewalks in the shape of children's mouths.

These silences I keep, they stutter, they stutter into speech and I find you, your voice, calling to the widow to come dance, come down here and dance mother, in the street, with us, you called to her, just around the corner

from the gold-domed Russian cathedral, where the widows kneel their heavy knees to pray in the shrouded peace of dark-faced icons.

What Song Is Singing in the Silence of the Snow

My Russian neighbors slumber, they lisp and sigh, they snore. They turn over towards what door. Open or closed, in the cathedral that is coughing, in the mine where they dig the ore that shines. That burns like coal, that heats the house of hems, the skirts that bloom in paisley, red, green, and blue as Ukrainian domes, as tattoos faded on the backs of ex-prisoners, sleeping before they wake for the early shift, and the sound of their cars sparking up in the dark, and the snow falling all around in hush. What music is left, this Prokofiev too much to bear, this Shostakovich that we share, piano keys that stutter charts, that mutter fields of dark earth, sunflowers, the digging and the ditch, the shovel and the spade, the cut above the shoulder blade, the ladder of a stitch, that leaves a scar, that when touched opens, opens a map of the body's archipelago, the islands of moles that stretch across the Northern sea of your back, and the snow ghosting against our bedroom window, choreographing its thousand falling stars.

Shell

For to forget him was to forget what was, which was, of course, she thought, a kind of beginning in itself, like an egg. Which didn't help, and she looked at her hands, and remembered how before sleep he would take her palm and tell her to close her eyes and guess, and then he would draw things there, starting simple with a heart, a figure eight, then more complex things, constellations (the Big Dipper), a horse-drawn carriage, a caboose (he was obsessed with transportation), a dictionary, a tree, a butterfly wing (which somehow she guessed), a baseball (she knew by the stitching he marked with his nails), a sombrero, Russian dolls, wooden puppets held by strings, and when they had filled her palms with mountains of tchotchkes (how many months had passed) he started with the images that merged to abstractions: wind through a rabbit's ear, a child eating a plum, a man waiting for a bus that never arrives, the color of evening light on a factory wall. "Like Hopper," she asked? "As if peering through a window at strangers," he answered. He laughed less, listened more. And how often she was correct, and yet she couldn't hear how he was becoming—transparent? She only thought later. The faintness of the yellow sheets they slept on. It was spring by then, a spring of hard rain and children plashing in puddles. The spring he couldn't find work, and often—more than not—she fell asleep with her hand blank in his. And then the nights he wasn't there, she touched her fingers to her palm, folded them and peered inside to see the dark egg, like a cave, heard it growing. And then he was gone. *It* was gone. She kept waiting for *him* to come back. She answered the phone at work, she walked. In the park, she found a robin's egg, broken and blue on the sidewalk, gathered up the shards, carried them home in the pocket of her purse. She took them out when she entered the empty apartment, spread them on the placemat he had bought. She leaned over them on the dining room table. On the tiny, white pieces of shell she scratched out with the head of a pin the secret hieroglyphics of her new life.

Naming the Wind

What wound of bread or lamp or pardon? Hear, when the wind is black. The streets are dark as if oiled. What name remembers the story of the snow? Last winter, when history was your eyes. Must it always be you, the sentence, the executioner of my still streets. The puddle's blackness or the pearl earrings worn by the Puerto Rican woman at the bar, in her black denims, and her hair cut short above her neck, and the scent of hyacinths and daffodils. Her eyes the color of plantains. What spins through the curfewed night, the teenagers glued to their antennas. Is this the wind that names what is holy, that sweeps like a broom through the last bar closing, the ashes of our dead or the ashtray the waitress dumps into the bin by the pool table, where the white man with the long white beard and one glass eye is searching his pockets for his keys. A key to open a door, a testimony. When laughter is a wound the lonely believe. Old Russian women with their rosary beads, their dark-faced icons, that sing when we sleep. That open their mouths and murmur the psalms. To sweep the dust from their holy ankles. Your ankle I'd hold in my palm and kiss. There is a dog barking out a secret anagram. A fire truck's silent siren spins, parked down the block. Someone has died or is nearly dead. What is whiter than a stretcher carried beneath the streetlights? When a stranger has turned over for the last time. Is there a name for this ache that fills us? And what is the name for this wind?

Jolie

Dusk drifts like a terrible scream. My friend Jolie is now a skull, or is she ashes? I can't recall. Only her freckled Lithuanian face alive, her mouth floating past Danny's pizza shop window on Seventh Ave. Her ghost has risen, whistling I used to *visit all the come what may places: Lush Life*, Billy Strayhorn's dark blue failure fingered, like a bullet struck into a bar stool. But that's not how she died, that's the bullet hole I found in the Parade Street bar where the boy was shot in the chest. The one I never knew. This is where she finds me, alone and wasted on too many vodka martinis. J died of cancer. A rare form. At thirty-three. You need to be direct sometimes. Pull out your tooth and count your griefs. Or do we call them losses? There is no translation for the bees, only the blossoms. The cherry blossoms pirouetting in the wind down the Eastern Parkway, where Jolie and Bill and I would walk, passed Hasidic families, the children's crazy mazurka across the colored-chalked sidewalk, their tassels trailing. In blue light of my stool I close my eyes. Jolie was nearly blind. When she met you, she would say, without irony, *You look good*. She felt us as a place in the air. The transitory obbligato of Being. The unfolding act of never being afraid. The way she reached for the chords on her guitar, their ecstatic Braille, the way her music made us raise our fists. When she said the word *revolution* it wasn't a theory: the way the yellow finches are singing the delicate light of her hair.

4

Poem That Ends in Purposeful Mistranslation

Skopje, Macedonia

the scarlet haze of the afternoon and the heads of strangers staring, their mouths spitting the Cyrillic alphabet. Is it harder or easier to feel anxious and paranoid in a country where you can't understand what people are saying? I walk to the river to toss my eyeballs into the muddy water, for some reason remember a terrible TV show *Malcolm in the Middle* as I watch Albanian men playfully punching a teenager smoking on the stone bridge rebuilt by the Ottomans do they read Malcolm, know the great American Muslim; Roger who last called me from a Tennessee prison bent his ear to Malcolm's words and found redemption in a concrete cell, the swirling is beginning to spell I can see him spinning two turntables and a mic and we are filling the blue smoky haze with an orange maze of pronouns that swirls and prowls like a leopard about to pounce to the ounce of cocaine on a plate before us and Michael the only one not high, all business balanced over the scales like the Department of Justice changed to *just us* flowing for so many of our brothers eclipsed ... hear the green-scarved Albanian women hustle hand-woven quilts, clock radios, pocket purses, the-gypsy-children–trained-in-weeping sit crossed-legged on the ground never look up as they reach out their hands. I am drowning in a language I can't even tell where the syllables stop and one word begins, when my friend touches my shoulder and says to me *dobro si* which means, more or less, *you are ok*, which I translate into what-is-the weight-you-are-carrying-my-Dear-One.

On Comes Light One

Skopje, Macedonia

Beso me so my body curls into a question, like after popping two pills and the sky opens umbrellas, beso me macaroon, magenta, indigo, and a cappella, beso me bad ass like blackjack or Cadillac or Billy Jack or Bruce Lee. Beso me like bribery. Beso me bruised and I will beso tu, your purple bush, your butterfly, I will lick your postage stamp. Beso me beeswax, clown-laugh, slingshot and swagger. Wager me, beso me, unsheathe my wounds, su beso un boca for coffins closing and cornmeal, for the rain sweeping across tin roofs, beso me into an arrival, the only destination your thighs, veed like the geese of autumn departing, beso me star-charted, languid-lapped, seamstress unsewing my lips, beso me half absentmindedly, mouth half open bad assed say to me, *come here bitch*, beso me Bella, bonita, señorita es rojo, beso me beyond our bodies, cull from my skin the lost sages, the laughter of grandmothers, the flour on their hands, white clouds we cough in the cafés where we scribble, beso me the bus driver's spare change, the orchestra plays riddles, rearranges the ruckus, the beautiful darkness instructs us at the edge of the square, so let's chase the gypsy boys pickpocketing passports to eat their laughter, why should they care the hospitals we've survived, the small rooms where we did not die, where we clung as if grieving, and our child crying, beso me without desire so I may hear her coo, that grew in you.

Untitled on Someone Else's Anniversary

she's crying again our child

you've been straight for two years

when you were high
the barbed wire

of our bodies

became hopelessly enbrambled
made her out of the dark

we smoked that winter

M called long past 3 AM
he was bleeding again

he isn't here to see her curls
or the cold rain washing the grit

on everything once clean

And the sickness that was us

was never

She is light

a flower could not capture

her elbow hard
against the black dog's rib

running she marries
our webbed hands

I have grown to fear

the silence I had been forgetting

is what I now hear
the shining music

of her chatter
the insomnia

she's sewn
into our eyelids

at dawn
never quite

disappears.

Scrawled Along the Crawling River

Skopje, Macedonia

What name means *hollow*

as the sound
I have traveled

away from you?
What name means *spilled spinach*

on the market ground,
the cough of exhaust,

and the commuters swaying
on the red buses,

pushed into one another,
into the absence of touch,

like the foreign arms of strangers?

What name means *basement pool hall*
where the tall Albanian kid, diesel

dark eyes, squinted,
aimed and sank the old factory

worker seven games:
the table's geometry

calculated by his cue:
What is the gerund for such precise joy?

The sky at the door

to the street
framed by the mountains

that hold the city
in their palms?

The river crawls
between the bankrupt's

unfinished architecture,
under the stone bridge

built by the Romans
where the man (younger

than me) with one good leg
and one dangling,

misshapen leg, hopped on crutches
carrying a plastic Tupperware tub

pleading for dinars.
His absent teeth,

the ones he used to sing through:
Albanian shirt sellers

ululating against the Ottoman centuries,
graffiti on the concrete embankment

written in an alphabet
I cannot read.

What name translates into
I have come to meet you

from my long sorrow?
What name means *the clouds*

are caravans
that migrate through my chest?

At dawn, I walk
the empty hallway,

the first sunlight
torches the mountains,

warms the wood floor.
I step naked into a rectangle

of light, a door
the width of a human body:

telling me the earth
is turning me towards you.

Undisclosed

On the morning it arrives

Will you cut open the sky

And find I have mailed myself to you

Like a letter bomb?

Duet

Why are you frowning? Unfold out your palms: you've trained me

You are quietly resting all morning on the window of what I did wrong: come look outside, I say, come hear what you've never heard:

You are all the way home I looked your way and you didn't become the music

You are not the I you say, I am: you are the orchard and the pool hall and the ink

You are somehow the one written who went before I could not spell what

You are saying, and the dealers outside shouting: and the rain scribbling curses against the screen

You are not the constellation of shotgun holes in the wall

You are and one of us will continue

You are the first time in a hotel room, Times Square long after midnight, the banished places the pimps were sent, the joint we shared by the basketball court, and the shard of glass you held up to the moon by the East River

You are unbuttoning my body

You are coffee and oranges in autumn, hushed recess: the sound of eating candy

You are alone the only voice that can keep me orphaned:

You are a saint's medallion in a small girl's hands

You are the one wrong joy transfigured

You are when there if there is nothing you tell me we can repeat
ourselves

You are barefoot running by the blue barn

You are somehow crayon singing:

U r the only letters of the alphabet uninvented

You are the last language I will ever learn

Notes

"Arias" was written for the Erie, PA poet Corey Zeller.

"The House of Fragments" employs a subjective collage technique derived from studying the collages of Romare Bearden. It attempts to tell a story through slippages and fragments, much as a collage makes a whole, an oblique narrative out of scraps, each one a concise element in the whole.

"At the Intersection of Parade and Punk": Gogol Bordello is a primarily Ukrainian founded gypsy punk band whose international nature, outlook, and refusal to compromise musical integrity offers us a path toward artistic community, celebration, and resistance in the 21st century.

"Our Love as an Origami Crane" mentions the great Icelandic singer Björk. The poem is written in a form I invented called the Fold Poem. In this form each end rhyme must repeat as the first sound at the beginning of the next line. The last word must rhyme with the poem's first word. This form is designed to generate strength and form on both sides of the line and to fold meaning and sound in a series of continuous progressions that makes a small tight unexpected form, much like a piece of origami.

"X" was written as a response to too many of my too careerist peers. I hope they listen and start to care more about saying what is so needed in these turbulent times rather than kissing up to the grant giving ruling class. Schoenberg is an Austrian-American composer who challenged and merged separate traditions of classical music and introduced atonality to a wider audience. Psychedelic Funk refers to the great George Clinton's band The Parliament who challenged separate genres of rock, soul, and funk. Their complementary ability to see behind and beyond genre and convention was a huge influence on my approach to writing.

"A J for Joe" is written after the poem "A W or M" by the great American poet (by way of Sweden) Malena Mörling. Jam Master refers to an old cut by the rap group RUN DMC. Johnstown refers to the great flood in 1889 that decimated the entire town of Johnstown, Pennsylvania.

"Shell": Hopper is the great American painter Edward Hopper.

"Jolie" is written in honor of my friend the great political folksinger Jolie Rickman, who died of cancer in 2004 at the age of 33. Billy Strayhorn is the great Jazz musician, who grew up primarily in Pittsburgh, PA and is best remembered for his collaborations with Duke Ellington. Here I refer to his devastating classic "Lush Life": "romance is mush / stifling those who try / I'll live a lush life in some small dive."

"Duet" is a performance poem written in two voices. I encourage you to read this poem out loud, improvising the splitting of the two voices, dividing them up in improvisations all your own.

Acknowledgments

Broome Review: "Subterranean Waltz," "After," "What We Were Given";
Bryant Review: "Shell;"
Hunger Mountain Review: "There is No Idea Here";
Indiana Review: "Scrawled Along the Crawling River";
Magma (UK): "At the Intersection of Parade and Punk";
New South: "My Neighbor Shadrack Is Coughing Again";
New York Quarterly: "The Opposite of Elegy," "On Comes Light One";
Parthenon West: "A J for Joe";
Seattle Review: "Ode and Elegy to the Sound of My Lover Peeing";
Slope: "Dear Tiara";
Whiskey Island Review: "Jolie."

Some of these poems were read on WJCU and WCPN in Cleveland, OH and on the radio in Skopje, the Republic of Macedonia, and Albanian Television in Tirana, Albania.

Special thanks to Peter Conners and Thom Ward and all the staff at BOA for their continued support and friendship. Great thanks to the Fulbright Fellowship Program sponsored by the United States State Department which helped support the writing of some of these poems. Thanks to the embassies in Skopje, the Republic of Macedonia, and in Tirana, Albania, for all your work on my behalf and on behalf of art and peace in the Balkans. Thanks to Suzanne and John for all their help with my beautiful son Gabriel. For Gabriel and his green-eyed grace. For Amara and her halo of amarillo. Thanks to my brothers in pool: Jim, Andy, Rick, Mikey, Brett, Clark, Sam, Andre, Bob, Mark the grand Sensei, and everyone at Gold Crown Billiards who studies the difficult art. Thanks to

Corey. Cody. Joe. Marc. Michele. Michelle. Paul M for the politics. Phil in Cleveland. Thanks to Zoran, Matt, Rumena, Paul, Jordan, Heidi, and Gordana in Macedonia. Thanks to the train station pool hall. Thanks to Jeffrey, Patricia, Lynn, Tim, Jen, Cindy, April, Tom, and Bill in NY. To Charlie and Roger in Chicago. To Peter, Terry, ML, Daniel Todd, and the crew in Detroit. To the Rochester Posse. For the Binghamton, Syracuse, and Erie diasporas. Dora and the same cosmic vibe. Sylvana my super soul sister. Thanks to ALL my Facebook crew, you know who you are and how you've kept me going when the dark was deep. Tacoma and Marc for the Music. Thanks for your kindness. Thanks most of all to the people of the East Side in Erie, PA where I lived and wrote and listened. Thanks to the Polish Falcons and the quarters and pool tables. Thank you Camel Cigarettes, Side One Dummy Records. Thank you all of you bad bad bad bad bitches.

About the Author

Sean Thomas Dougherty is a self-described "underground sound."

Editor's Note: Sean Thomas Dougherty is the author of eleven books and his awards include a Fulbright Lectureship to the Balkans from the US State Department and two Pennsylvania Council for the Arts fellowships in poetry. Known for his electrifying performances, he has performed widely across North America and Europe. Though currently, his exact whereabouts are uncertain, as he wrote to us in his last correspondence, "it is time to once again disappear into the streets that are singing and weeping with human voices."

BOA Editions, Ltd.
American Poets Continuum Series

No. 1 *The Fuhrer Bunker: A Cycle of Poems in Progress*
W. D. Snodgrass

No. 2 *She*
M. L. Rosenthal

No. 3 *Living With Distance*
Ralph J. Mills, Jr.

No. 4 *Not Just Any Death*
Michael Waters

No. 5 *That Was Then: New and Selected Poems*
Isabella Gardner

No. 6 *Things That Happen Where There Aren't Any People*
William Stafford

No. 7 *The Bridge of Change: Poems 1974–1980*
John Logan

No. 8 *Signatures*
Joseph Stroud

No. 9 *People Live Here: Selected Poems 1949–1983*
Louis Simpson

No. 10 *Yin*
Carolyn Kizer

No. 11 *Duhamel: Ideas of Order in Little Canada*
Bill Tremblay

No. 12 *Seeing It Was So*
Anthony Piccione

No. 13 *Hyam Plutzik: The Collected Poems*

No. 14 *Good Woman: Poems and a Memoir 1969–1980*
Lucille Clifton

No. 15 *Next: New Poems*
Lucille Clifton

No. 16 *Roxa: Voices of the Culver Family*
William B. Patrick

No. 17 *John Logan: The Collected Poems*

No. 18 *Isabella Gardner: The Collected Poems*

No. 19 *The Sunken Lightship*
Peter Makuck

No. 20 *The City in Which I Love You*
Li-Young Lee

No. 21 *Quilting: Poems 1987–1990*
Lucille Clifton

No. 22 *John Logan: The Collected Fiction*

No. 23 *Shenandoah and Other Verse Plays*
Delmore Schwartz

No. 24 *Nobody Lives on Arthur Godfrey Boulevard*
Gerald Costanzo

No. 25 *The Book of Names: New and Selected Poems*
Barton Sutter

No. 26 *Each in His Season*
W. D. Snodgrass

No. 27 *Wordworks: Poems Selected and New*
Richard Kostelanetz

No. 28 *What We Carry*
Dorianne Laux

No. 29 *Red Suitcase*
Naomi Shihab Nye

No. 30 *Song*
Brigit Pegeen Kelly

No. 31 *The Fuehrer Bunker: The Complete Cycle*
W. D. Snodgrass

No. 32 *For the Kingdom*
Anthony Piccione

No. 33 *The Quicken Tree*
Bill Knott

No. 34 *These Upraised Hands*
William B. Patrick

No. 35 *Crazy Horse in Stillness*
William Heyen

No. 36 *Quick, Now, Always*
Mark Irwin

No. 37 *I Have Tasted the Apple*
Mary Crow

No. 38 *The Terrible Stories*
Lucille Clifton

No. 39 *The Heat of Arrivals*
Ray Gonzalez

No. 40 *Jimmy & Rita*
Kim Addonizio

No. 41 *Green Ash, Red Maple, Black Gum*
Michael Waters

No. 42 *Against Distance*
Peter Makuck

No. 43 *The Night Path*
Laurie Kutchins

No. 44 *Radiography*
Bruce Bond

No. 45 *At My Ease: Uncollected Poems of the Fifties and Sixties*
David Ignatow

No. 46 *Trillium*
Richard Foerster

No. 47 *Fuel*
Naomi Shihab Nye

No. 48 *Gratitude*
Sam Hamill

No. 49 *Diana, Charles, & the Queen*
William Heyen

No. 50 *Plus Shipping*
Bob Hicok

No. 51 *Cabato Sentora*
Ray Gonzalez

No. 52 *We Didn't Come Here for This*
William B. Patrick

No. 53 *The Vandals*
Alan Michael Parker

No. 54 *To Get Here*
Wendy Mnookin

No. 55 *Living Is What I Wanted: Last Poems*
David Ignatow

No. 56 *Dusty Angel*
Michael Blumenthal

No. 57 *The Tiger Iris*
Joan Swift

No. 58 *White City*
Mark Irwin

No. 59 *Laugh at the End of the World: Collected Comic Poems 1969–1999*
Bill Knott

No. 60 *Blessing the Boats: New and Selected Poems: 1988–2000*
Lucille Clifton

No. 61 *Tell Me*
Kim Addonizio

No. 62 *Smoke*
Dorianne Laux

No. 63 *Parthenopi: New and Selected Poems*
Michael Waters

No. 64 *Rancho Notorious*
Richard Garcia

No. 65 *Jam*
Joe-Anne McLaughlin

No. 66 *A. Poulin, Jr. Selected Poems*
Edited, with an Introduction by Michael Waters

No. 67 *Small Gods of Grief*
Laure-Anne Bosselaar

No. 68 *Book of My Nights*
Li-Young Lee

No. 69 *Tulip Farms and Leper Colonies*
Charles Harper Webb

No. 70 *Double Going*
Richard Foerster

No. 71 *What He Took*
Wendy Mnookin

No. 72 *The Hawk Temple at Tierra Grande*
Ray Gonzalez

No. 73 *Mules of Love*
Ellen Bass

No. 74 *The Guests at the Gate*
Anthony Piccione

No. 75 *Dumb Luck*
Sam Hamill

No. 76 *Love Song with Motor Vehicles*
Alan Michael Parker

No. 77 *Life Watch*
Willis Barnstone

No. 78 *The Owner of the House: New Collected Poems 1940–2001*
Louis Simpson

No. 79 *Is*
Wayne Dodd

No. 80 *Late*
Cecilia Woloch

No. 81 *Precipitates*
Debra Kang Dean

No. 82 *The Orchard*
Brigit Pegeen Kelly

No. 83 *Bright Hunger*
Mark Irwin

No. 84 *Desire Lines: New and Selected Poems*
Lola Haskins

No. 85 *Curious Conduct*
Jeanne Marie Beaumont

No. 86 *Mercy*
Lucille Clifton

No. 87 *Model Homes*
Wayne Koestenbaum

No. 88 *Farewell to the Starlight in Whiskey*
Barton Sutter

No. 89 *Angels for the Burning*
David Mura

No. 90 *The Rooster's Wife*
Russell Edson

No. 91 *American Children*
Jim Simmerman

No. 92 *Postcards from the Interior*
Wyn Cooper

No. 93 *You & Yours*
Naomi Shihab Nye

No. 94 *Consideration of the Guitar: New and Selected Poems 1986–2005*
Ray Gonzalez

No. 95 *Off-Season in the Promised Land*
Peter Makuck

No. 96 *The Hoopoe's Crown*
Jacqueline Osherow

No. 97 *Not for Specialists: New and Selected Poems*
W. D. Snodgrass

No. 98 *Splendor*
Steve Kronen

No. 99 *Woman Crossing a Field*
Deena Linett

No. 100 *The Burning of Troy*
Richard Foerster

No. 101 *Darling Vulgarity*
Michael Waters

No. 102 *The Persistence of Objects*
Richard Garcia

No. 103 *Slope of the Child Everlasting*
Laurie Kutchins

No. 104 *Broken Hallelujahs*
Sean Thomas Dougherty

No. 105 *Peeping Tom's Cabin: Comic Verse 1928–2008*
X. J. Kennedy

No. 106 *Disclamor*
G.C. Waldrep

No. 107 *Encouragement for a Man Falling to His Death*
Christopher Kennedy

No. 108 *Sleeping with Houdini*
Nin Andrews

No. 109 *Nomina*
Karen Volkman

No. 110 *The Fortieth Day*
Kazim Ali

No. 111 *Elephants & Butterflies*
Alan Michael Parker

No. 112 *Voices*
Lucille Clifton

No. 113 *The Moon Makes Its Own Plea*
Wendy Mnookin

No. 114 *The Heaven-Sent Leaf*
Katy Lederer

No. 115 *Struggling Times*
Louis Simpson

No. 116 *And*
Michael Blumenthal

No. 117 *Carpathia*
Cecilia Woloch

No. 118 *Seasons of Lotus, Seasons of Bone*
Matthew Shenoda

No. 119 *Sharp Stars*
Sharon Bryan

No. 120 *Cool Auditor*
Ray Gonzalez

No. 121 *Long Lens: New and Selected Poems*
Peter Makuck

No. 122 *Chaos Is the New Calm*
Wyn Cooper

No. 123 *Diwata*
Barbara Jane Reyes

No. 124 *Burning of the Three Fires*
Jeanne Marie Beaumont

No. 125 *Sasha Sings the Laundry on the Line*
Sean Thomas Dougherty

Colophon

Sasha Sings the Laundry on the Line, poems by Sean Thomas Dougherty, is set in Sabon, a digitalized version of the typeface designed in 1964 by the German typographer Jan Tschichold (1902–1974.) The display type is Myriad Pro.

The publication of this book is made possible, in part, by the special support of the following individuals:

Anonymous x 2
Jan & Ken Bailey
Aaron & Lara Black
Gwen & Gary Conners • Mark & Karen Conners
Peter & Karen Conners
Wyn Cooper & Shawna Parker
Charles & Barbara Coté in memory of Charlie Coté Jr.
Peter & Suzanne Durant
Robert L. Giron • Kip & Debby Hale
Janice N. Harrington & Robert Dale Parker
Bob & Willy Hursh
Robin, Hollon & Casey Hursh in memory of Peter Hursh
X.J. & Dorothy M. Kennedy
Jack & Gail Langerak • Elissa & Ernie Orlando
Boo Poulin
Boo Poulin in memory of Debra Audet
John F. Roche
Deborah Ronnen & Sherman Levey
Steven O. Russell & Phyllis Rifkin-Russell
Vicki & Richard Schwartz
Gerald Vorrasi • Ellen Wallack
Dan & Nan Westervelt in honor of Patricia Braus & Edward Lopez
Pat & Mike Wilder
Glenn & Helen William